LOVESPOONS
FROM WALES

Dr. D. C. PERKINS

Photographs by Michael Corrin

Illustrations by Alison Fewtrell

CW00953969

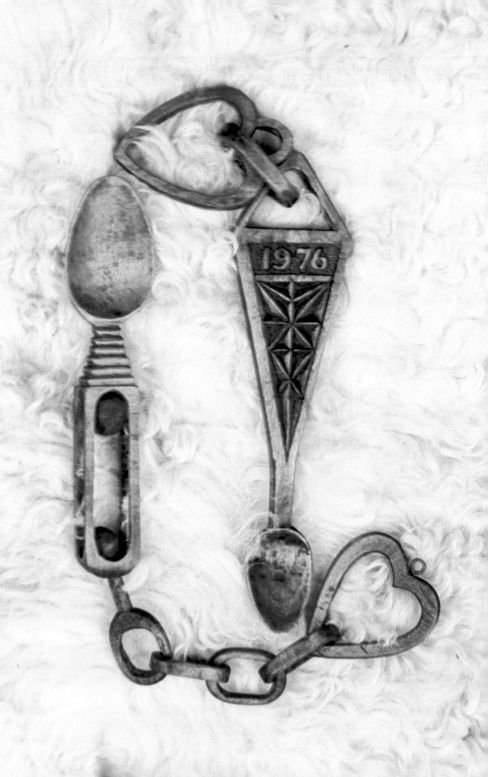

FOREWORD

Lovespoons were given by suitors to their sweethearts in Wales from the 17th. to the early 19th. century. The custom of giving lovespoons died out in the 19th. century but they continued to be carved especially in some country districts. Making lovespoons became something of an art form and woodwork competitions and Eisteddfodau often had examples of the *genre*.

In recent years, interest in lovespoons has reawakened and many people seek them out as desirable keepsakes. Visitors to the Principality, particularly from overseas, wanting something uniquely Welsh to remind them of their visit, often choose a lovespoon. There is also a growing tendency for Welsh people themselves to give lovespoons as gifts to commemorate special occasions - a new baby, a birthday, an impending marriage, a retirement or to celebrate a success of some kind. Lovespoons also make excellent Christmas presents. Today, when most people have neither the time nor the inclination to carve their own lovespoons, the accepted practice is to buy a ready-made example of the craft or to commission one of the woodcarver specialists to make one.

DCP

© DCP and EJP, 1989
6th. impression, 1995

Domino Books (Wales) Ltd
P O Box 32, Swansea SA1 1FN
Tel. 01792 459378   Fax. 01792 466337

LLWYAU CARU
LOVESPOONS

Since pre-history, beautiful, hand-carved objects have had ceremonial, romantic and religious significance: long incense and cosmetic spoons, for example, have survived from Egyptian times. In the Middle Ages, a pair of knives in a sheath was considered a worthy gift and it was common for a bridegroom to present his bride with one: such sets were known as 'wedding knives'.

The history of kitchen utensils and the spoon belongs to Western culture. The history of the lovespoon belongs to Welsh romantic folklore.

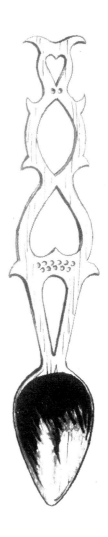

From the mid-17th. century, lovespoons were carved from wood in Wales and there is one dated 1677 in the collection at the Welsh Folk Museum, St. Fagan's, Cardiff. It is amazing that this has survived because wooden objects are not particularly durable and little was known about the preservation of wood when this 17th. century item was made.

It is not clear when the distinction between spoons designed for culinary use and those with romantic associations emerged. The practice of making all sorts of kitchenware (including plates, bowls, cups and saucers and eating utensils) pre-dates lovespoon use by centuries. Culinary spoons, *llywau pren* and soup or *cawl* spoons were made in most Welsh

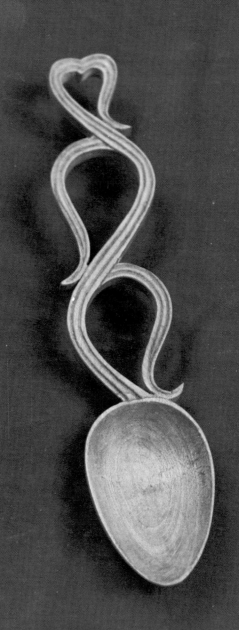

households.

From the 17th. century, the custom grew for a young man to give a spoon to the lady who took his fancy. Thus, particularly attractive young ladies might be given a number of spoons from aspiring suitors. It may be that the modern word, 'spooning' indicating a closer development of a relationship, is derived from this practice of giving a love token.

Early lovespoons were carved from sycamore which was readily available in the low-lying country districts of the Principality. The main tools used were a pocket knife for whittling the wood and a *twca cam* for hollowing out the bowl. Those who made such spoons were amateurs and it was a way of passing the time on long winter evenings. Imagine a young man busily shaping a spoon in a small room lit only by candlelight or the glow of a fire.

Numerous examples of lovespoons have been found throughout Wales but the giving and receiving of a spoon did not develop into 'a ritual of betrothal'. Indeed, there is strong evidence to suggest that giving a lovespoon expressed a desire for a relationship and was not an affirmation that a relationship had already begun. This was not the case elsewhere. For example, the Bretons make similar spoons but they call them 'marriage spoons' and on the wedding day a bridegroom carries or wears a spoon.

I have written elsewhere that the *lovespoon*

evolved from the culinary spoon and *from the utilitarian use the lovespoon developed symbolical significance** but it is obvious that once established, the culinary spoon and the lovespoon developed side by side.

Some young men did not have the time or the skill to carve their own spoons and professional lovespoon carvers emerged. It was again, a question of demand and supply. Spoons were bartered for or purchased from these skilled craftsmen and a tradition of spoons made by the same wood worker grew in the 18th. and 19th. centuries. It was no wonder then, that the spoon became more decorative and elaborate.

A number of design factors should be mentioned in relation to spoon carving including size, weight, colour and the nature of the completed artefact.

As far as size is concerned, the earliest spoons were little bigger than the modern teaspoon, their use was limited, and larger spoons soon came to be carved. This meant that the handles, in particular, could be more and more elaborate. As they became more decorative, the spoons were displayed by hanging them on the wall in the living room or parlour. The weight and type of wood used for such a spoon depended on the setting in which it was to be displayed. Softwoods

*See 'The Story of the Lovespoon' published by Emeralda (Welsh Mills) Ltd.

were often preferred and the colour selected so that it would look good against a wall.

A great deal of imagination was used in the creation of lovespoons. This elaboration was gradual. Two or even three bowls were carved instead of one to make it more interesting and attractive. Eventually, the bowl became less important and attention turned first to the handle and then to embellishments or additions to the handle.

Sometimes the handle was enlarged or made rectangular in shape. At other times, filigree was added. The handle was pierced, cutting designs in fretwork, carving in relief or escalloping the edges were devices to add interest and meaning to the spoon. In this way, symbols were incorporated: hearts, locks, keys, shields, anchors and wheels were favoured themes.

A heart or a series of hearts was the most popular expression of love used on spoons. These might be single or entwined to suggest that the boy and his girl would soon feel the same way about each other. As the spoons became more decorative, their utilitarian use ceased altogether and they were used more for display. The heart was also an attractive and convenient device for suspending the spoon on a wall or Welsh dresser. Indeed, most spoons have a device for hanging them up, indicating that they were decorative rather than functional.

Anchors in particular were popular: the suitor has found a berth where he wished to stay. Many lovespoons were the work of seafarers who whiled away the tedium of a voyage by whittling. Besides anchors, ropes and cable designs often appear, as do vessels, steering wheels and various other nautical emblems.

Locks (keeping love or a lover safe), keys (unlocking love), miniature cottages and houses are recurrent themes with associations of lovers making a life together. The key may have a triple significance for it may indicate unlocking the door to the heart, it may indicate maturity (reaching 21 and the key to the door theme) or it may mean here is the key, let's live in marriage together.

The significance of a sphere or ball captive in a cage in a handle has been variously described. One suggestion is that the sphere denoted a soul imprisoned in a cage of love, another is the symbolical meaning that the ball (the suitor's heart) has been captured by the lady and cannot escape until his love is returned. Yet another, is the message of security: the loved one will be kept safe. The spheres may also have represented or predicted the number of children that could be expected from the union: a bigger ball may have indicated a boy and a smaller one, a girl. But perhaps this is reading too much into the design and the spheres may just have been a way a carver showed

his skill. Like *the ship in the bottle, the ball in a cage* carving almost always elicits the query, *How did you get it in there?* The uninformed find it difficult to believe that such a handle could be made from one piece of wood.

Chain links look very difficult to carve and are another development of the whittler's art showing the woodworker's skill. Suggestions are that the links symbolically *link* the sweethearts together in love and possibly matrimony. Unfortunately, historically, chains have other unhappy connotations and the symbolism should not be taken too far especially when remembering the harsh penal system in 17th. and 18th. century Wales.

The soul motif, shaped like a comma, on a spoon may have been intended to emphasise the sanctity of a forthcoming union. Lovers knots may symbolise the bond between lovers while flowers, roses, or rosettes suggest that, like plants, love if nourished, will also flourish.

This growth theme is emphasised by the vine. As the plant strengthens, so will the suitor's love while the entwining of the vines symbolises holding - the longing to hold the object of one's love in one's arms.

Some spoons are intended to be in the nature of Valentines and to be anonymous. (It is difficult to understand that someone who had spent many hours creating such a gift would not want his work to be appreciated.) Others are bolder with dual initials, those of the suitor and his lady or a single initial when we are left to guess whether this represents the donor or the donee.

Nationalistic emblems such as a daffodil, a leek, the word *Cymru** or even a dragon are sometimes used, but these move away from the traditional themes and are usually seen on modern spoons

Overpage is a list of of some of the themes found on lovespoons. But we must try not to read too much into the minds of the carvers of earlier days. Whatever we think, we cannot help being amazed by the consummate skill of these lovespoon craftsmen.

*Curiously, cariad (darling) is rarely seen on traditional lovespoons.

THE SIGNIFICANCE OF LOVESPOONS AND THEIR MOTIFS

It must be stressed that many assumptions have been made about the meaning/s of the motifs which appear on lovespoons. Imagery is always difficult to explain and certain motifs may have had more personal significance for the donor than can be appreciated by the casual observer. Spoons were not mass-produced but made by one individual for another and many relied on personal nuances other than symbols to convey meaning. For ease of reference, the motifs are given in alphabetical order.

Motif	Possible Meaning/s
Acanthus leaf	Our love will grow.
	Love grows if nurtured.
	Let us cultivate our love.
Anchor	I want to stay with you.
	I want to live with you.
	I want to be with you.
	We should marry and settle down.
Anchors(2)	Our destinies are similar.
	We should stay here and live together.
	This is where we should stay.
Ball	We shall have a child.
See spheres also	Our union will be blessed.

Motif	Possible Meaning/s
Ball *cont.*	Love held safe.
Bell/s	Signifies a wedding.
	Joyfulness for love returned.
	Let us make music together.
Bird/s	Let us elope.
	Come away with me.
	We are two love birds.
	Birds of a feather flock together.
Chain	Our destinies are linked.
	We should get together.
	Our lives are linked together.
	We should never be separated.
	Together for ever.
Cross	Let our union be sanctified.
	Together in Christ.
	Faith binds us together.
	Let us marry in church.
	God blesses us.
	God will bless our marriage.
Crossed Keys	Home and security.
	Let us pool resources.
	Key to my heart.

Motif	Possible Meaning/s
Crossed ' Keys *Cont.*	May I have the key to your heart?
Daffodils *See flowers also*	Our love will grow. Symbol of love. Symbol of affection. Symbol of Wales. Let us live together in Wales.
Diamonds	Riches together. We shall be enriched together. Love me and this will make me wealthy.
Doublespoon *two bowls*	Let us be together. Togetherness.
Flowers	Our love will grow. Shows my affection. A gift of love.
Feathers	We shall be like birds in a nest. Marry me and make a home (a nest). Comfort together. Symbol of Wales (Ich Dien).
Fruit	Fulfilment of wishes. Fulfilment of love.

Motif	Possible Meaning/s
Heart	My heart is yours.
	Your heart belongs to me.
	You have won my heart.
	Do not break my heart.
	My heart's desire - you.
	Chastity.
	Steadfast love.
Hearts	We belong together.
	Our hearts should beat as one.
	Give me your heart and I shall give you mine.
	Do not be fainthearted - love me as I love you.
	Love is returned.
Heartshaped bowl	A full life together.
	A happy life together.
	We shall be happy together.
Horseshoe	Good luck in love.
	Good luck in marriage.
	Love me for good fortune.
	Work and live together for good luck.
Initials	Denote the object of affection.
	One set - the first names of the donor or donee.
	Two sets - let us join together.

Motif	Possible Meaning/s
Key/Keyhole	My heart is yours.
	Maturity.
	Let us live together.
	My house is yours.
Lantern/s	I like what I see.
	I should like to see more of you.
	Reciprocated love will bring light to my life.
	I will light your path.
Leek/s	Love grows strong.
	Symbol of strength of love.
	Symbol of Wales.
Link	We cannot be separated.
	Our love cannot be broken.
	Our destinies lie together.
	We are inseparable.
Lock	I shall look after you.
	Security.
Lovespoon	The spoon itself has a symbolical significance as a whole. It suggests the desire for a relationship.
Ship	Smooth passage through life.

Motif	Possible Meaning/s
Ship *Cont.*	Seeking a safe harbour.
	Searching for love.
Ship's Wheel	Be my guide.
	Let me guide you through life.
	Let us guide each other through life.
Spade	I will work for you.
	I will work to gain your affection.
	Let us live and work together.
Spectacles	I like what I see.
	I wish to see more of you.
	Can't you see I love you?
	Do not miss my affection for you.
Spheres	Love held safe.
See balls above	Our union will be blessed.
	We shall have a child or children (as indicated by the number of spheres).
	Boy child - bigger sphere than a girl child.
Soul Sign	Our union will be blessed.
	Our love affair will be sanctified.
	God blesses us both.
	God is love.

Motif	Possible Meaning/s
Treblespoon	We will make a nice family.
three bowls	Our love will be blessed.
	Let us live in harmony.
Twisted Stem	Our lives are inseparable.
	We cannot live apart.
	We belong together.
	Whoever God joins together,
	let no man put asunder.
Vase	Our love must be nurtured.
	Love will grow.
	Love needs to be sustained.
Vine	Our love will grow.
	Love grows stronger daily.
	Our love affair will be blessed.
	Our love will bear fruit.
	Growing together.
	Fertility.
Windows	To see the loved one clearly.
	To look after the loved one from a distance.
	I am watching over you.

Dated and Personalised Spoons

Some spoons are dated. If the couple eventually marry, they then become a keepsake of the suitor's original interest. Other spoons are personalised either by initials or by an emblem of the occupation or the interests of the donor or donee.

Often a carver wishes to incorporate a date, a monogram, a motto, a name or a quotation into a carving. If he wants to keep it a secret, he may work the date or name into the design.

A LOVESPOON GLOSSARY

Acanthus: this leaf was the motif of many designs by Roman carvers and appears in some early lovespoons.

Artisan: a skilled craftsman or workman.

Awl: a pointed hand tool with a fluted blade used for piercing wood or leather.

Axe: a hand tool with one side of its head sharpened to a cutting edge and used not only for felling trees but also for splitting timber.

Ball in a Cage: carving one piece of wood so that a sphere is made which is trapped by the surrounding wood.

Caricature: in wood, a representation of a person which exaggerates his or her traits or foibles for comic effect.

Chisel: a hand tool used for working wood. It consists of a flat, steel blade with a cutting edge attached to a handle of wood or plastic. It is either used by hand or struck with a mallet.

Chisel cut: cutting with the outer edge of a blade and forcing it through the wood without a sawing action.

Cleavability: the ease with which wood splits for use.*

Drill: a hand tool operated either manually or electrically and used for making holes.

George Hepplewhite:
died 1786   famous English woodcarver and cabinet maker who specialised in oval- or shield-shaped open chairbacks.

Grinling Gibbons:
1648 - 1721   probably the greatest of all woodcarvers. He was was noted for his delicate carvings of fruit, flowers and birds.

Hardwood: describes dense woods which are difficult to work and carve. Examples are oak, ash, beech and walnut.

Hatchet: a short axe used for chipping and splitting wood.

Hone: either a tool used to give a smooth finish to wood or the art of smoothing and finishing wood.

Knife-craft: an alternative name given to whittling. Working with a knife, especially as an art form.

*Hard to split are elm, sycamore, beech, holly, birch and hornbeam. Medium to split are oak, ash, larch and poplar. Easy to split are chestnut, pine, spruce, fir and cedar.

Loveknot;
Lover's Knot: a stylised bow made of ribbon or other material which symbolises the bond between lovers.

Lovespoon: a utensil made of wood given to a woman as a token of the feelings a man has for her. In the form of a spoon, it had a symbolical meaning.

Mahogany: a wood, red or brown in colour, close and even in grain. It is fairly hard, easy to work and is very suitable for carving.

Mallet: a tool resembling a hammer but having a large head of wood used for driving and working a chisel.

Nested Spheres: carvings in which one or more spheres or balls are placed inside each other.

Présentoirs: in mediaeval times and later, this was the name given to serving knives made in pairs. They were used solely for passing food.

Pyrography: the art or process of burning designs on wood or leather with heated tools or a naked flame.

Rasp: a coarse file used to smooth wood or edges.

Robert Adam: Scottish architect skilled in furniture design.
1728 - 92

24

Rocking Cut: one of the eight principal ways of whittling. It implies a backwards and forwards movement of a knife or blade over the cutting edge.

Rose: a design or decoration shaped like a flower.

Rosette: a decoration or pattern resembling a rose especially an arrangement of ribbons or strips formed into a rose-shaped design and worn as a badge. Some lovespoons have a rosette design on the handle.

Rosewood: close-grained, very hard and beautifully figured wood. It ranges in colour from bright red to deep purple and the East Indian variety may be deep brown, black or even yellow. It has a roselike scent and is used to make lovespoons and in borders and inlays.

Saw: a hand tool having a blade with teeth along one edge and used to cut wood or metal.

Saw Cut: a motion similar to sawing used in cutting through the last piece of wood holding a chain link or a ball-in-a cage.

Scraping Cut: using a knife or blade for removing bark from a piece of wood.

Soft Woods: open-grained wood of numerous coniferous trees. They

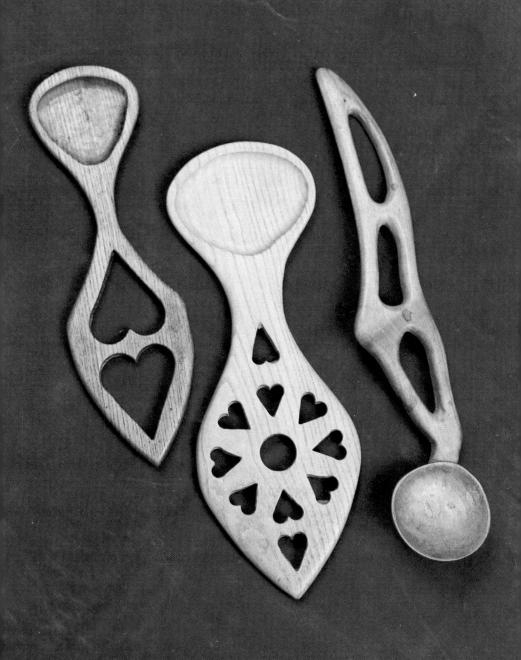

include chestnut, Douglas fir, pine, larch and spruce.

Split:

cleaving wood into separate pieces, often into two roughly equal pieces. Wood hard to split is elm, sycamore, beech, holly, maple and birch. Medium to split is oak, ash, larch and poplar. Wood easy to split is chestnut, pine, spruce, fir and cedar.

Straight Cut:

one of the eight principal ways of whittling. This cut simply implies removing waste wood.

Stop or Outline Cut:

one of the eight principal ways of whittling. This is made by pulling the knife blade along a line, thus cutting into the wood along the line and preventing later cuts from splitting past the outline.

Sweep Cut:

One of the eight principal ways of whittling. This is swinging the knife about the cutting edge of the blade as it moves forward, giving a curved cut with a smooth outline.

Thomas Chippendale: *?1718 - 79*

English cabinet-maker and furniture designer. He used He used massive carvings with Chinese and Gothic motifs.

Thomas Sheraton: *1715 - 1806*

English cabinet-maker. Author of the influential tial 'Cabinet Maker' and 'Upholsterer's Drawing Book' (1791).

Treen; **Treenware:**	the name given to small articles such as lovespoons and other items made of wood.
Trencher:	a wooden board or plate on which food was served or cut.
Twca Cam:	a tool resembling a bent scythe used in Wales in early days to shape utensils and hollow out spoon bowls.
Very Soft Woods:	these include balsa, basswood, pine, redwood and willow.
Whittle:	to cut or shave pieces of wood with a knife, especially with a view to making and shaping an object or objects.
Whittlings:	chips or shavings cut off from an object made of wood.
Woodcarving:	the art of carving wood, especially as an art form. It also means the article produced by carving wood.

FROM THE SAME PUBLISHERS

Visit Wales, An Annual Guide.

The Welsh Pantry, Recipes

Country Cooking, Recipes from Wales

Celtic Recipes

Coffee Morning, Recipes

Afternoon Tea, Recipes

Cooking with Herbs and Spices

Wonderful Herbal Remedies

West Country Cooking

West Country Teas

Wales, Its Customs and Cooking

Dylan Thomas and His World

Customs and Cooking from Scotland

Scottish Cooking

Scottish Teas

Scottish Place Names and Their Meanings

Welsh Place Names and Their Meanings

London Place Names and Their Meanings

Cockney Rhyming Slang

Conferences Welcome, A Guide

Business Letters Made to Measure

Details from

Domino Books (Wales) Ltd. P O Box 32, Swansea SA1 1FN.

Tel. 01792 459378 Fax. 01792 466337

Publishers of **MASTER FILES** for the NATIONAL CURRICULUM

A MAJOR RESOURCE FOR TEACHERS AND PARENTS